Los jardines cambian

por Karen Baicker

Scott Foresman
is an imprint of

PEARSON

Glenview, Illinois • Boston, Massachusetts • Chandler, Arizona
Upper Saddle River, New Jersey

Photographs

Every effort has been made to secure permission and provide appropriate credit for photographic material. The publisher deeply regrets any omission and pledges to correct errors called to its attention in subsequent editions.

Unless otherwise acknowledged, all photographs are the property of Pearson Education, Inc.

Photo locators denoted as follows: Top (T), Center (C), Bottom (B), Left (L), Right (R), Background (Bkgd)

Opener: Tetra Images/Alamy
1 ©blickwinkel/Alamy Images
3 ©Peter Gerdehag/Jupiter Images
4 Getty Images
5 ©Edd Westmacott/Alamy
6 ©blickwinkel/Alamy Images
7 ©Tetra Images/Jupiter Images
8 ©Ariel Skelley/Getty Image

ISBN 13: 978-0-328-47426-4
ISBN 10:   0-328-47426-6

Copyright © by Pearson Education, Inc., or its affiliates. All rights reserved. Printed in the United States of America. This publication is protected by copyright, and permission should be obtained from the publisher prior to any prohibited reproduction, storage in a retrieval system, or transmission in any form or by any means, electronic, mechanical, photocopying, recording, or likewise. For information regarding permissions, write to Pearson Curriculum Rights & Permissions, One Lake Street, Upper Saddle River, New Jersey 07458.

Pearson® is a trademark, in the U.S. and/or other countries, of Pearson plc or its affiliates.

Scott Foresman® is a trademark, in the U.S. and/or other countries, of Pearson Education, Inc., or its affiliates.

2 3 4 5 6 7 8 9 10 V010 18 17 16 15 14 13 12 11 10

El jardín tiene nieve.

El jardín tiene semillas.

El jardín tiene hojas.

El jardín tiene flores.

El jardín tiene calabazas.

¡El jardín tiene niños!